Can I Forgive God?

CAN I FORGIVE GOD?

Leslie F. Brandt

CONCORDIA PUBLISHING HOUSE
Saint Louis London

Concordia Publishing House, St. Louis, Missouri
Concordia Publishing House Ltd., London, E. C. 1
Copyright © 1970 Concordia Publishing House
Library of Congress Catalog Card No. 74113077

MANUFACTURED IN THE UNITED STATES OF AMERICA

Contents

Preface 7

Chapter 1. Can I Forgive God? 13
2. Can God Forgive Me? 25
3. Can I Forgive Myself? 35
4. Can I Forgive Others? 43
5. Can I Forgive Those
   I Love the Most? 53
6. Can I Forgive —
   And Celebrate? 61
7. Can I Forgive —
   And Serve? 69

Preface

On a cold winter day in March 1947 my wife, my small daughter, and I were deposited by airport bus somewhere in the middle of Peking, China. After weeks of waiting in Shanghai, we finally found passage to our final destination, where we were to spend a year or so at the College of Chinese Studies in Peking.

No one had seen us off; no one was there to meet us. If there had been any English-speaking passengers on the bus, they vanished the moment the bus stopped. In a period of 3 minutes the only human beings left were a group of chattering ricksha runners trying to sell their services to us. I had been taught a series of incomprehensible sounds that were supposed to lead us to our destination in that city. I tried them out on the runners about us. They chattered, grinned, flailed their arms, stuffed us into their flimsy vehicles, pulled down a canvass to block out cold and vision, and took off into the heart of that strange and beautiful metropolis.

I was in one ricksha, my wife and daughter in another, and our baggage in the third. As I could not be sure of the other two rickshas, I kept verifying their proximity through intermittent calls and yells as we trundled along over the rough cobblestones. It soon became apparent that the runners had not understood my initial attempt at speaking Chinese. Every 2 or 3 blocks we came to a jolting halt. One of the runners would disappear into a shop and emerge with somebody in tow. I would repeat my series of sounds to that person; he would stare, shake his head, and walk away. After the fourth stop I was becoming frightened. I had never felt so lost in my life. It was getting dark. We were all feeling the cold. I was having visions of our being cornered in some dark alley and stripped of our possessions.

Our little armada pulled out into a windswept intersection and headed for the other side. In the middle of the street, with trucks, oxcarts, and bicycles milling about us, the runners stopped short and called out to some pedestrian in the vicinity and pointed him to my ricksha. I pulled aside my canvass and, eyeball to eyeball, recited my little incantation. He grimaced, shook his head, then turned to me and said in perfect English: "Where do you want to go?"

It reminded me of the Word of a loving God breaking through to a man lost in sin. I was found again; I was secure. He translated my English into something the runners could comprehend, and off we went. I still had some apprehensions as we rumbled through narrow streets and still narrower alleys, between high stone walls topped with broken glass or barbed wire; but I retained the confidence that we were going in the right direction. Suddenly we stopped; the canvass was pulled away from our faces, and we found ourselves before a walled-in institution that bore the title, in English as well as in Chinese, "College of Chinese Studies." All was well. We were "home."

The message of this little volume is not new, and yet it is ever new and precious. Scores of writers have been far more articulate than I in proclaiming what I am trying to communicate. And yet it is possible that I may say something that will give point and purpose to someone who may be lost in the intricate, chaotic morass of this disjointed world.

What I have tried to say, in essence, is that there is meaning in life and purpose for living. One can discover and retain his identity even amidst the fears and frustrations of this uncertain, day-by-day existence. It is spelled out for us in the forgiveness of a loving God and demonstrated to us through the teachings and activity of Jesus Christ. When we have caught on to what it means to live in forgiveness, we will know who we are and where we are going. What is more, we will then become creative and contributive in our interpersonal relationships with our fellowmen about us.

The world about us, like some strange and foreign city, is ever exciting and foreboding. The child of God is ever exposed to its threats and dangers. But he is never alone, and he is never lost. He has a path to walk, a destination to reach, and a God who accepts and loves him. If someone can learn something more about this path, this destination, and our great and loving God through these pages, I shall be ever grateful.

Leslie F. Brandt

1

Can I Forgive God?

DURING A SCENE in Eugene O'Neill's play *All God's Children Got Wings,* one character asks another, "Will God forgive me?"

"Maybe He can forgive you for what you have done to me," the second replies, "and maybe He can forgive me for what I've done to you, but I don't see how God can forgive Himself."

I haven't dared to phrase it that way, but I have questioned God's integrity in the face of all the misery that exists in the world today.

I questioned it when I came across starving children rummaging for goodies in the garbage heaps of Shanghai.

I questioned it when I read Thomas Dooley's *Deliver Us from Evil,* which outlines his experiences in attempting to piece together the bodies of human beings torn apart by communist atrocities.

The philosopher Hume once wrote, "Were a stranger to drop suddenly into this world, I would show him, as a specimen of its ills, a hospital full of diseases, a prison crowded with malefactors and debtors, a field of battle strewn with carcasses, a fleet floundering in the ocean, and a nation languishing under tyranny, famine, and pestilence."

I could show him a few 20th-century atrocities that would turn his stomach: the victims of fate or chance in mental institutions, the deformed children born into our already distorted world, the blood spilled on our highways as well as our battlefields.

Can I forgive God? Is God helpless before the ruthless surge of evil today? I have little difficulty concerning affirmations of God's existence, but how can I continue to affirm that God is LOVE?

I asked the question when the jolting news of my pastor-father's violent death reached across the nation to flatten me in despair. "O God, why . . .?"

I asked it as I watched my beautiful young friend slowly yield her vitality to the ravishes of an ugly tumor that encircled her spinal cord and snuffed out her life. "O God, why . . . ?"

I ask it in my monthly visits with a young man who is paralyzed from the neck down. "O God, why . . . ?"

"But through the hurt seeps the healing of heaven," I bravely wrote concerning my father's sudden demise. "Whatever Satan's insidious intent, there is the incomprehensible conviction that God sat beside Dad in that fateful moment and transformed that which was designed for evil into an agent of His own eternal purposes. . . . He would not have chosen this manner of his passing, but he was ready for the fact and the event. Death for him was not an accident, but an incident that transmitted him from the incompleteness of this existence into the fullness and the totality of God's presence."

I wrote it—and I believed it. I believed in the inscrutable purposes of God as I sang "Precious Lord, Take My Hand" to my young friend the evening before she died. And I continue to believe in God's grace and purposes as I listen to the young man who can move only his head and his lips confessing his impatience with his male nurses and praying for divine grace to help him communicate God's love to workers and patients about him. But even while I believe, I am haunted by the apparent contradictions that face me at every turn in the road.

I find little comfort in the assertion that God does not WILL suffering; He only permits it.

I am aware that four fifths of the suffering in our world is caused by the folly and wickedness of its inhabitants. It is man, not God, who makes racks, whips, knives, guns, nuclear warheads, and death-dealing bacteria that can wipe out the human race in a matter of hours. And it is man, not God, who pollutes our air and water and ravages our natural resources.

I am also aware of the contribution

that my own self-centeredness and insensitivity make to the distortions of this world.

I live with suffering. I am, at almost every moment, in the midst of some conflict. This is how it is, and this is the way I am. This is the world in which I live.

I identify with the disciples in what we now regard as a rather stupid question when, in the face of human distortion, they asked of Jesus, "Rabbi, who sinned, this man or his parents, that he was born blind?" I still find it difficult to warm up to the answer of Christ, who said, "It was not that this man sinned, or his parents, but that the works of God might be made manifest in him." And yet it is Christ's answer that provides a basis for a living faith. It offers no logical explanation to the problem of suffering. It does, however, offer hope to those who accept the world as it is and who will dedicate their lives to the alleviation of human suffering wherever it may be found.

It is no longer a matter of whether

or not I can forgive God. It is a matter of living productively in this world, even with its disorder and distortions. God is here to judge its wickedness and at the same time to minister to its ailments. When I accept this world and God's presence within it, I am enabled to communicate God's presence and power in the midst of its atrocious pains.

During Katherine Mansfield's long struggle with illness, she wrote in her journal, "I do not want to die without leaving a record of my belief that suffering can be overcome, for I do believe it. What must one do? Do not resist it. Take it. Be overwhelmed. Accept it fully. Make it a part of life. Everything in life that we really accept undergoes a change. So suffering must become love."

One of the well-known seven words from the cross was that word emitted by our Lord at the very peak of His agony, "My God, my God, WHY . . .?" This has often been my screaming question in the face of the little crosses that have come my way or the heavy crosses laid upon those whom I love.

I am not really foolish enough to blame God for my pains and problems; I am human enough, as was Jesus Himself, to ask, "Why?" But I am not about to stop with that query and live the rest of my life under the shadow of that twisted question mark. Our Lord's life was not snuffed out under a question mark. Before He ebbed His last breath, He turned this apparent tragedy into the basis of universal blessing with the prayer of victory, "Father, into Thy hands I commit My spirit."

There were three crosses on Calvary. They represent three different attitudes towards suffering.

One cross was the cross of the thief who complained bitterly about his plight, lashing out in rebellion as he approached the hour of death.

Another was the cross of the thief who repented of his wrongdoing and sought God's mercy in this 11th hour of his life.

Then there was the cross of Christ. In that cross I find the Christian answer to suffering. Jesus did not ignore pain and sorrow and suffering. Nor did He seek to be exempted from it. He embraced it and used it and through this event made it possible for men dead in sin to be brought back to life again.

In Ingmar Bergman's famous but cynical and despair-laden production *Winter Night*, one of the characters shares with his pastor his thoughts about Christ's crucifixion. It was his opinion that our Lord's greatest suffering was not the physical pain of the thorns or the nails or the heavy cross. It was the moment of doubt that came even to the human Christ concerning His Father's love for Him. He sensed it only for a moment, but it was the moment of His greatest suffering.

Can I forgive God? Of course I can't forgive God—simply because He IS God, Almighty, All-righteous, and All-loving. My need is to accept Him and relate to Him in the midst of this world's catastrophes, to acquiesce to its agonies, to open my heart and mind to receive whatever muted messages they may bring my way. While I do so, I will never need to endure the frightening, soul-destroying agony of God's rejection.

2
Can God Forgive Me?

THE MOST DIFFICULT speech I have ever made is confined to three simple words, "I am wrong."

If I cannot get along with someone, the reason usually lies in his peculiarities.

If I fail in some project, it is not myself but some outward circumstance that is to blame.

When the work of the church fails to bring forth new converts, I look for the reason in others.

If the placid waters of family relationships are disturbed, I can quickly discover something within my mate that needs correcting.

I am an escapist by nature, running for my life, at least when it comes to the place where the honor of self is at stake.

Only after I have investigated

every other possibility do I reluctantly invade the entrenchments of self. There I generally find the real reason for fruitlessness, disunity, or unhappy relationships.

Sooner or later I bite the dust. I am cornered by my very own faults and failures, and I shamefully come out of my hole to confess, "I am wrong." I am told that this is the way back to God, the way of repentance. If it is not already too late, it may be the way back to renewed relationships with church, community, home, and family.

The point of recognized failure is a low point in my life. It is as if the bottom has dropped out. The psalmist knew the meaning of failure: "Save me, O God," he cried, "for the waters have come up to my neck. I sink in deep mire, where there is no foothold; I have come into deep waters, and the flood sweeps over me. I am weary with my crying; my throat is parched. My eyes grow dim with waiting for my God."

With the pain of failure comes the

plague of guilt. It burns like a fire within me and influences the way I think and act. The smoke and fumes which rise from this hidden fire choke off my effectiveness and fog up my relations with others. I try desperately to cope with it. I become resentful. I may even find myself pinning my guilt feelings on someone else and then punishing him or finding some distorted form of relief in the hurt of others. Most of the time I employ a self-accusatory mechanism and slink about like a dog with its tail between its legs.

The great message of the Gospel is that "God has concluded all under sin, that He might have mercy upon all." Stewart James writes about the "incomparable experience of forgiveness." He points up how in their search for happiness through kicks and thrills, wealth or pleasure, the pathetic inhabitants of our chaos-ridden globe have little inkling that the incomparable experience of life is found in a man's restoration to God through acceptance and forgiveness by Him.

But can God forgive me? The natural law is unrelenting. What a man sows, that shall he also reap. As a man makes his bed, so he must lie in it. As a man acts, so he must bear the consequences of his act. This is what the many voices inside and outside of me are shouting. And more often than not, I listen to them.

There is something I must learn again and again. The experience of forgiveness becomes more incomparable every time I deal with it. It is the grand truth that the grace of God slices through all the condemnatory and judgmental accusations and promises of the Law. The good news of the Gospel is that forgiveness is possible. God can and does forgive me. Natural law may rule the universe, but God is personal Spirit and creative Love, and God says: "I have swept away your transgressions like a cloud, and your sins like mist." "As far as the east is from the west, so far does He remove our transgressions from us."

Can God forgive me? The New

Testament clearly declares that God has forgiven me. It happened over 2,000 years ago. Jesus Christ took my guilt on Himself and went to the cross. By His crucifixion He died for the world and with an overpowering force shattered that vicious and stifling bondage in which the human race was helpless. It is too deep to fathom, too profound to comprehend, but when Christ suffered on Calvary, it was God who suffered on behalf of His human creatures and in that hour broke through every barrier to make a way for sinful man to come back to Him.

This is the good news of forgiveness. It means that I no longer need to continue lying bound within the soul-destroying power and paralysis of unforgiven sin. My sins—past, present, and future—were removed in that amazing act of God in A. D. 30. God through Christ entered the arena of our conflict and disease at Christmas. He won the battle over evil and its ugly consequences at Easter. He returned at Pentecost to inhabit the heart of man with supernatural power to confront and overcome sin. It is a fact accomplished. It is done. God HAS forgiven me.

The words "I am wrong" are prerequisite to being made right again. The words "I believe" are the condition to realizing that rightness.

The utilization of these words in no way alters or enhances the validity of that crucifixion on Calvary so long ago. Nor does the failure to utilize these words in any way negate that act.

It is entirely possible to starve to death even if there are a million dollars in my name in some trust fund that I have never heard about or refuse to acknowledge. If I fail to appropriate the money which is mine, I remain poverty-stricken.

The great act of Christ on Calvary has cleared my name and opened the gates for my return to God. But I can never, at least in this life, know the security of God's eternal love and the glorious freedom of sonship unless I appropriate His incomparable gift of forgiveness by rising up to walk and to serve within this new life of love and joy.

I don't have to go down the sawdust trail every time I fall or fail. I do have to be keenly aware of my humanity and its self-centered taints and tendencies and be open before God and man.

I don't have to recite some incantation or creed in the endeavor to be reinstated in God's favor. I do have to stand perpetually on God's promises and assurances as they are revealed in His Word.

I am His. I belong to Him. His gifts are not extended or withdrawn in accordance with my "badness" or my "goodness." He does not expell or suspend me from His kingdom when I fail to measure up to His standards of discipleship. But the power of His love has no equal, and it continues to draw me ever more deeply into His purposes and, in spite of my fallibilities, enables me to experiment with ever greater degrees of sacrificial love toward humanity about me.

Can God forgive me? I can't always feel it, but I can believe in God's forgiveness because He said it and demonstrated it through Jesus Christ. When I persistently anchor my life on the facts of God's eternal love for me, the feelings ultimately catch up to those facts, and I know the joy of God's love and acceptance of me even in the midst of conflict.

Can God forgive me? It is my failures and imperfections that make me eligible for His loving grace revealed in Christ and communicated to me through the Word and the sacraments. He shares His love and power with me as I respond in faith to His Word and sacraments. God can and does forgive me.

3

Can I Forgive Myself?

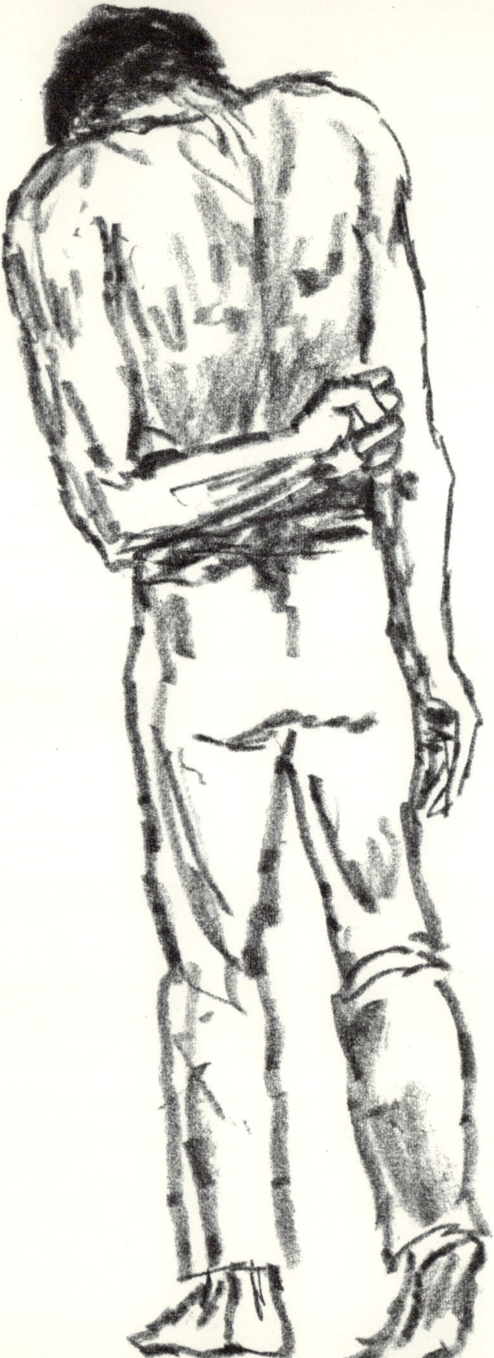

A WEAVER IN ENGLAND prayed this unusual prayer: "O God, help me always to keep a good opinion of myself."

I could not have subscribed to this presumptuous piece of arrogance a few years ago. I assumed, as I had been brainwashed to believe, that to be virtuous or pious I had to think negatively about myself.

Jesus once told a parable about a servant whose master relieved him from an impossible-to-pay debt. Incredible as it seems, this same servant immediately sallied forth to beat up a fellow servant who was indebted to him. The first servant was forgiven of his debt; but this did not alter the resentment and hostility in his heart, and he turned right around to take it out on his fellowman.

I couldn't understand this kind of reaction in the early years of my life. I think I do now. I have been told by psychologists that unresolved hostility is one of the major sicknesses of the human psyche. Anger affects the sympathetic nervous system and may produce actual physical illness. A small child may have a gastric upset as the result of a temper tantrum. Headaches often follow anger. Persistent colds are sometimes attributed to anger and resentment. Asthma is occasionally blamed on repressed hostilities. People have killed themselves because of hostile feelings. I read about a man who was in good health up to the time he became enraged over a lawsuit his sister brought against him. It obsessed him; he could think or talk of nothing else. His appetite failed. He lost sleep and weight. His heart and kidneys developed malfunctions. Before many months passed, he was dead.

Some of the hostilities that bother us may be the result of exaggerated self-esteem. There have been times when

I resented what others did to me because I thought overmuch of myself. But I discover more often that the hostility I feel is really a projection of my own self-hatred or self-deprecation expressed toward or inflicted on others.

In counseling people whose personality profiles are marked "hostile" or "critical," I have generally discovered deep feelings of inferiority and invalidity. A dominant husband is often a very insecure employee on the job. He plays a role at home which is dramatically different from the way he acts when he is with the boys at the plant or the office. A critical or nagging wife often hacks away at her mate or the members of her club in the attempt to bring others down to the level of her small feelings about herself. On the other hand, I have occasionally dealt with a wife who returns to her brutish husband again and again even after he repeatedly beats her within an inch of her life. More often than not, I discover in these clients a deep sense of inferiority coupled with guilt.

These people basically have a very poor opinion of themselves.

Someone once said that "when a king picks up a trifle, it is a trifle no longer." The fact is God sent His Son to pick me up. He loves, understands, forgives, and accepts me. He has reconciled and reunited me to Himself. It is this that gives me identity and validity. I am no longer the slave of self and sin, but the very son of God. It took a good deal of positive thinking and a series of therapeutic sessions to convince me, but I am learning how to discard the picture of myself as a fear-haunted, guilt-stricken, sin-ridden nobody and am now able to hold up my head. Because it is a false picture, it must go.

God has accepted me as His son and commissioned me as His servant. I am somebody! I may not always feel like such, but I must continually put aside the fiction of foolish feelings for the facts of God's proclamation. "We are called God's children, and such we are," said John. Then I must step out into this world to live and serve as such, believing with Paul that "God is at work in us, both to will and to work for His good pleasure."

I know that God can and has forgiven me. Now the question is: Can I forgive myself? What is it with this inborn prejudice toward other races or social classes, this bigotry, this snobbishness, this looking-down-my-nose at the weaknesses and failures of others? Does it not scream out to the world my own feelings of inferiority and the fact that something is radically wrong with my relationship to God? I know He has forgiven me—but do I really believe it?

It is when I do really believe it, when I accept God's acceptance of me, that I am able to forgive myself. It is then that I realize in truth what I previously put on like a facade, that I am valid, significant, worthwhile and authentically important. It is then that the English weaver's prayer makes sense, for even I can have "a good opinion of myself." It is then that I can pray like a modern psalmist: "I thank You,

O God, for making me valid and significant, for putting meaning into my life and purpose into my living, for snatching me out of the pit of self-centeredness and restoring my identity as a member of Your eternal family."

Can I forgive myself? I can — and I must. If God through Christ can forgive and forget forever my atrocious faults and failures, who am I to usurp His loving mercy and short-circuit His proffered grace by refusing to accept His acceptance of me? My sins have been wiped out. My significance has been established forever by His appointment to Kingdom duties and responsibilities. I am the son and servant of the living God.

4

Can I Forgive Others?

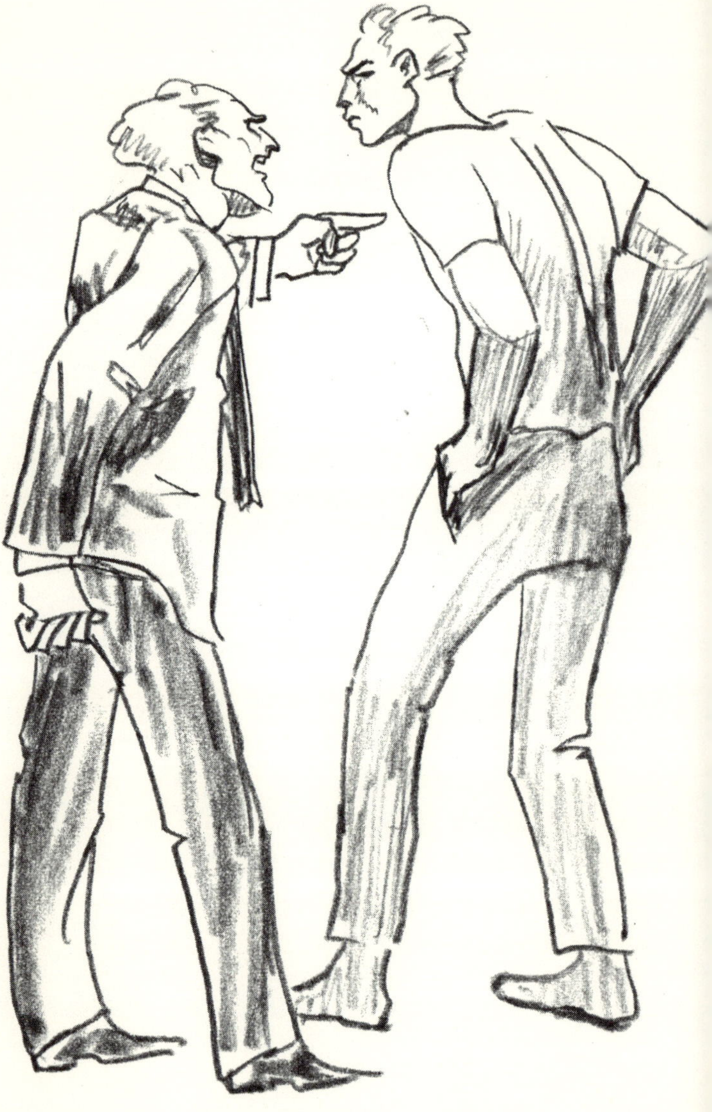

I REMEMBER READING about an Armenian nurse who accepted and nursed back to health the very Turk who had killed her brother. When wounded and desperately sick, this Turk was brought to the hospital and placed under her care. Overcoming natural hate with Christ-inspired love and concern, she eventually led him to embrace the Christian faith.

A Korean pastor asked the Court to entrust to his care a young communist who had been condemned to death for the brutal murder of this pastor's two sons. Obtaining the consent of the Court, the pastor took this young man into his home in place of the sons he had lost, and this murderer eventually became a Christian.

I read and I remember, but I find it almost impossible to identify with or to emulate the kind of love demonstrated by these very special saints of past and present. I am more likely to echo the sentiments of the psalmist who made no bones about drawing the line between his friends and his enemies and even dared to call down God's wrath on those who persecuted him. "Awake, O Lord," he cried, "in Thy anger; lift Thyself up against the fury of my enemies." "Arise, O Lord! Confront them, overthrow them! May their belly be filled with what Thou hast stored up for them. . . ." "Let them be put to shame and dishonor who seek after my life! Let them be turned back and confounded who devise evil against me! Let them be like chaff before the wind, with the angel of the Lord driving them on! Let their way be dark and slippery, with the angel of the Lord pursuing them! Then my soul shall rejoice in the Lord. . . ."

There were other psalmists, of course, who did speak about the forgiveness of God. Nevertheless, I cannot rest my case totally upon the meditations of these ancient songwriters. The real life-style for me is manifested and demonstrated by the Word-made-flesh, Jesus Christ, and by the Armenian nurses and Korean pastors who are caught up in Christ's Spirit and infilled with His power.

Can I forgive others? Can I forgive a church member who calls me a communist? a son who shuns the moral values in which he and I have been brought up? a spouse who can't respond to some of my childish needs? a friend who turns his back when I need him?

Can I forgive the husband who leaves his family without any support? the reckless driver who runs down a child? What about infidelity, addiction, cruelty? Can I—should I—forgive the perpetrators of such atrocities?

I can and I must. This is what Jesus did and declared in His ministry on this earth. His love-your-enemy, do-not-resist, turn-the-other-cheek, go-the-second-mile style of life is often most impractical. It is His style of life nonetheless, and His injunction to those whom He invited to follow Him.

His words are clear. "So if you are offering your gift at the altar, and there remember that your brother has something against you, leave your gift there before the altar and go; first be reconciled to your brother, and then come and offer your gift." "Lord, how often shall my brother sin against me, and I forgive him? As many as seven times?" asked Peter. "I do not say to you seven times, but seventy times seven," responded Jesus. "For if you forgive men their trespasses, your heavenly Father also will forgive you; but if you do not forgive men their trespasses, neither will your Father forgive your trespasses." "And forgive us our trespasses as we forgive those who trespass against us."

The old marriage vows for the bride read "love, honor, and obey." Someone suggested a modern alternative for both parties: "love, honor, and forgive." It is interesting to speculate on how much the divorce rates could be cut down if "forgiveness" were as much a part of the marital relationship as, for instance, the conjugal bed. "For your hardness of heart Moses allowed you to divorce your wives," said Jesus to the Pharisees, and "hardness of heart" is very close to hell itself.

It is disconcerting to realize how often my unforgiving attitudes toward others are in reality a reflection or a projection of my disgust for myself. My recognition and declaration of my own bankruptcy, and of God's acceptance of me as I am, certainly ought to result in making me tender, acceptive, understanding, and forgiving toward my fellowman.

It does not mean that I must condone his failures and distortions any more than I am expected to condone my own. But I must learn how to tolerate the weaknesses he has not yet learned to transform into strength or the liabilities he has not yet turned into assets. I need, for my sake and for his, to accept and love him as a valid, significant, worthwhile person even in the midst of his faults and failures.

As a creation of God, my fellowman is as close to God as I am, and just as continually in need of His grace. We belong to the same club—the brotherhood of sinners. Through loving acceptance one of the other, we can contribute toward the salvation and sanctification of the other and grow together into vehicles of usefulness and effectiveness.

Not only must I forgive others: I must be aware that such forgiveness is genuine. It is so easy to assume a role, to put on a front, to adopt a facsimile of the real thing and to project a condescending, holier-than-thou sort of attitude. True forgiveness is not a degrading or demoting of the person I am to relate to. I must not, even unconsciously, seek to take away his stripes or reduce his rank. I must, instead, accept him as my equal, a brother in Christ.

Can I forgive others? I can—with

God's enabling grace, and I must. This is the life-style of a Christian who is commanded and empowered to "love his neighbor as himself."

5

*Can I Forgive Those
I Love the Most?*

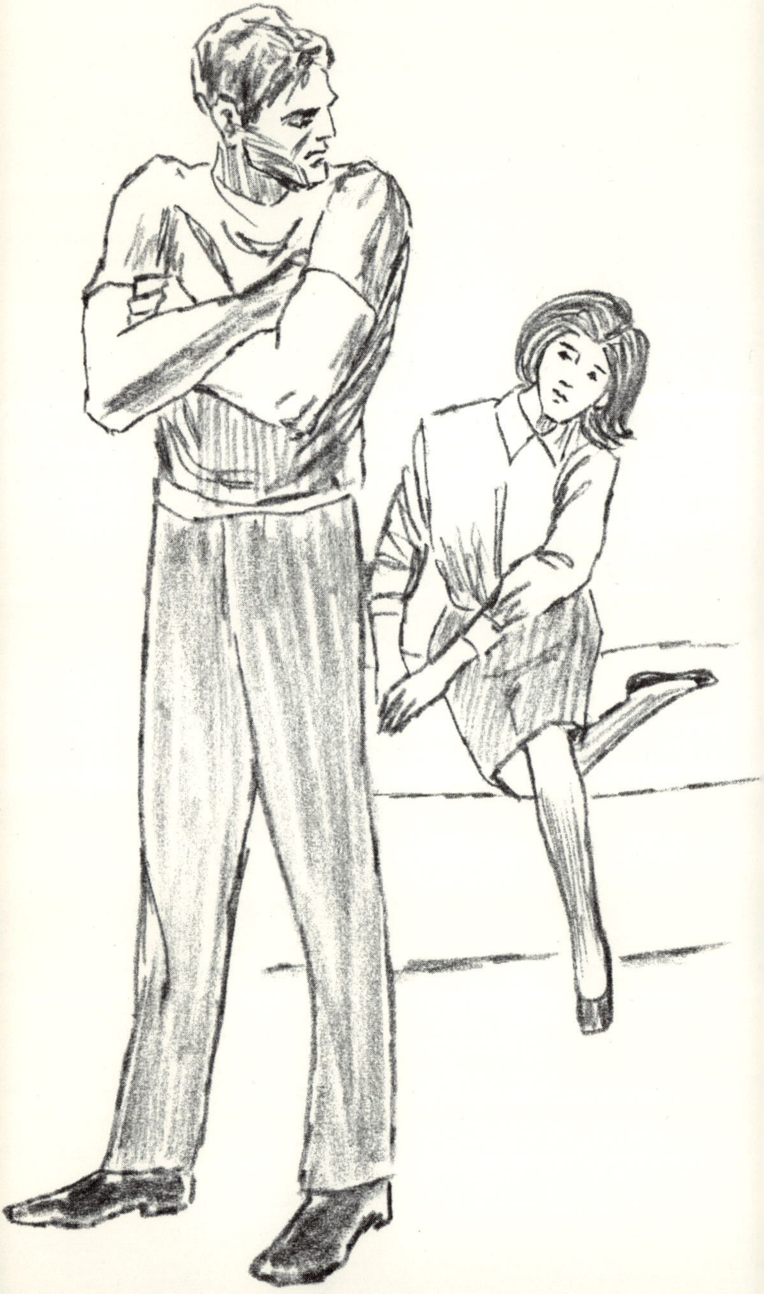

I CAN MAKE GRANDIOSE STATEMENTS about my willingness to forgive or to tolerate the atrocities of my fellowmen, and may even demonstrate it among less intimate relationships about me. But when it comes to my most personal relationships—with those I love the most—my willingness or ability to forgive is often in question.

This is not as strange as it may appear. Parents who have given their offspring everything material they have asked for will sometimes disown their sons if they grow beards or experiment with drugs, or their daughters if they become pregnant before marriage. Young men have been banned from their homes because they have chosen prison rather than subscribe to military service. Mothers and fathers have announced to the creatures they have borne and brought up that either they adhere to the religious, moral, and cultural standards set up for them or else they never want to see them again. Sadly missing in these instances are the love and concern that Jesus constantly expressed to people about Him, as well as His hopeful view of the possibility of repentance and a better life.

Marital breakups that never even reach the counselor's office are sometimes instigated by one mate who suspects or discovers the other mate is involved in some extramarital relationship. Staunch, moral people often assume that such activity immediately and by necessity terminates a husband-wife relationship.

The message of a father who lovingly awaits the return of a prodigal son, of Christ's tender dealing with a woman caught in the act, of God's persistent reach for His wandering children is lost on many religious people today. Much of the chaos and unhappiness about us comes out of the unwillingness or inability of people to forgive those whom they love the most.

Christ's injunction is to "go after the one who is lost." He backed it up with action in His loving acceptance of harlots and publicans and those who were haughtily scorned by the religious people of His day. It is regrettable but more easily understood when religious people shun the problematic sinner, but how can they, or I, explain our difficulty in forgiving those whom we love the most?

The most obvious explanation is that my professed love for my intimates is generally an adulterated love. In spite of the affection shown or the gifts given, the professions and the proclamations, my love is self-centered rather than sacrificial. I love in response to love. Instead of loving others as myself, I love myself in others. I seek, unconsciously or otherwise, to possess those whom I profess to love. I find myself guilty of drawing my ego-strength from them. I am sometimes more of a leech than a lover. When those who are dear to me reach out to take from or give to others, it frightens me. I react in jealousy with hurt feelings and hostility. Instead of contributing to the independence and personhood of others, I unwittingly seek to rob them of what they have. I tend to treat those close to me as things rather than persons. I will live, even die for them, support and protect them, as long as they live within my structures and walk according to my strategies and respond to my childish needs.

All this is reflected in most human love-relationships, but the kind of love manifested and projected by Jesus Christ is very different and represents the kind of interpersonal relationships that lead to personality health and happiness.

Jesus demonstrated a selfless, living-for-others kind of love that bears little resemblance to the "passionate partiality" that Kierkegaard refers to and which typifies the kind of attitude or activity I am most likely to reflect toward those I love the most. There may be as much immorality within marital relationships as in any other area of life. It is hidden from the general public but becomes obvious in the resultant marital fractures that keep pastors and marriage counselors busy today.

Can I forgive those whom I love the most? Only if my love for those who are close to me is an authentic love. This does not mean that I must condone my spouse's weaknesses nor, like Eli in the Old Testament, be perpetually permissive toward the children under my care. It does mean that I love them irrespective of the flaws and failures in their lives. It means that I must allow my peers, even my children, the right to make mistakes, to fail, and continue to be lovingly open and acceptive to them. The joys of true love are often interrupted with hours of agony, the kind of agony Jesus must have experienced as He witnessed the calloused indifference of those, even within His own family, whom He came to bless and to save.

This kind of love or ability to love is not the natural possession of any man, but it is available to every man. It comes by way of the forgiving and saving love of God as lived and presented in Jesus Christ. When I am absorbed in and by God's redeeming and regenerating love, I should be enabled to reflect such love in my interpersonal relationships. Though God's gift of love is immediate and all-inclusive, I learn very slowly, even with the prompting of the Holy Spirit, how to truly love those I love the most. Learn I shall, slowly and surely; and as I learn to love, I will most certainly learn how to forgive those whom I love the most.

6

*Can I Forgive —
And Celebrate?*

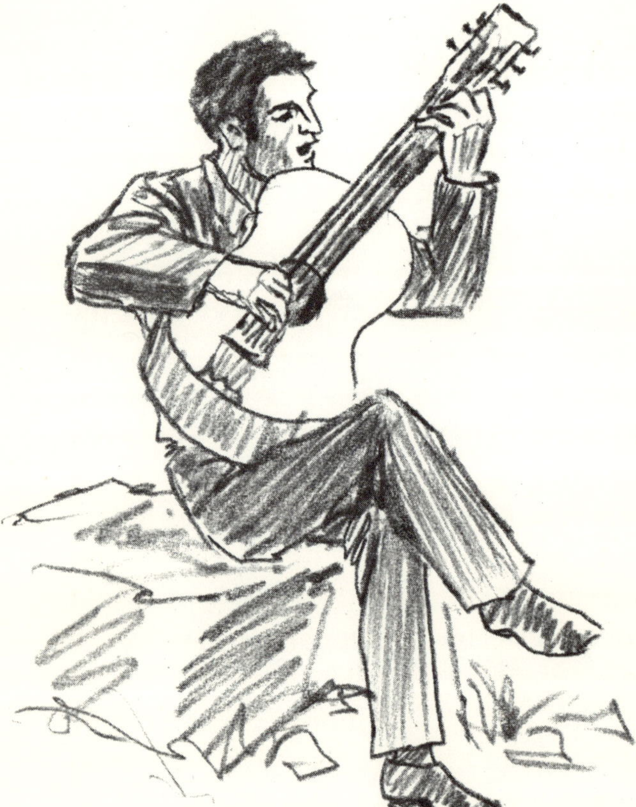

"And we are writing this that your joy may be complete," said John. Then he proceeded, in his First Letter, to talk about forgiveness.

Many circumstances about me tend to stifle joy. Most of them may eventually be compromised or overcome. The factor which most surely takes the joy and bounce out of my life is guilt. It has to do with something that stands between me and my fellowman—and therefore between me and God. Can I forgive—and celebrate? "How many crimes are committed because their authors could not endure being wrong?" questions the chief character of Albert Camus' *The Fall*.

The fact is, I cannot really celebrate unless and until I forgive. Any happiness I may experience while unforgiven or unforgiving is ephemeral and short-lived. It bears no resemblance to the joy the Scriptures talk about.

Divine forgiveness means total release from the guilt of sin and failure in my life. An integral part of this forgiveness and most essential to this release is my forgiveness of myself and my fellowman. When God forgives, and this resolves in my forgiving, I am set free to celebrate.

What I remember most clearly about the religion of my youth is that it was predominately occupied with condemnations and warnings against sin. The teachings of my religious superiors seemed to weigh most heavily on the "don'ts" of the Christian life. There were cloud-nine experiences from time to time, but celebration was little emphasized and too much of it was considered somewhat impious. Forgiveness means that I am set free to celebrate. Celebration is one of the most important aspects of worship.

Celebration, for me at least, hasn't always taken place in the church sanctuary or to the tunes and rhythms of traditional liturgies.

Sometimes it followed a spat with my spouse when all was forgiven and reconciliation took over.

It happened to me while I conversed with my black friends on a Chicago street.

I celebrated when I played games with my fellow pastors on a Pacific beach.

I have celebrated with a patient dying of cancer in a hospital who knew she was soon to be totally reunited with God.

I have celebrated in the serene beauty of the San Bernardino Mountains, where I sometimes go to write and meditate.

The most enriching and often most ecstatic moments of celebration have been with groups of God's servants, whatever their race or their denomination, in the language school at Peking, China, the Urban Training Center in Chicago, with friends in their cabin in Minnesota, a therapy group in Los Angeles, and with individuals with whom I have had an open and loving relationship.

We celebrated together because we were keenly conscious of God's loving acceptance of us despite our human flaws and hang-ups and because of our loving, forgiving acceptance of one another.

What is there to celebrate in our distorted world? In the face of almost unsolvable problems such as racism, war, overpopulation, and pollution—how dare we celebrate? How can I celebrate my good fortune while my brothers and sisters throughout the world and even in my own neighborhood are hungry or oppressed or the victims of some illness or tragedy?

I don't think I dare to celebrate my good fortune unless I am able and willing to dedicate it to the needs of my fellowman. What is given to me is lost unless it is passed on to others. But God's forgiveness and acceptance, and my resultant ability to forgive and accept others, grants me the privilege

CAN I FORGIVE — AND CELEBRATE? 67

and the responsibility of celebrating His presence in our world today.

God is here — let's celebrate! He is here in the hearts and lives of those who are open to Him and to each other. He is here to heal and to hallow, to redeem and sanctify, to love and to forgive His every creature. Celebration is our faith in and our witness to this eternal truth.

A contemporary version of one of the psalms explodes in these words:

> *God is here, let's celebrate!*
> *With song and with dance,*
> > *with stringed instruments and brass,*
> > *with cymbals and drums,*
> *Let us express our ecstatic joy in God's presence.*
> *Let us celebrate with the old songs of praise.*
> *Let us also create new songs that portray the eternal love of our God.*
>
> *God continues to create and to conquer, to renew and to redeem the world about us.*

He does this through those who relate to Him,
   who rely on His ever-present love.
He delivers His children from the fear of death
   and through them gives life to this world.

God's love is sure and everlasting.
The hearts that are open to His love are filled with joy.
They truly find cause for celebration.

Can I forgive—and celebrate? There is no real joy apart from forgiveness. And this forgiveness which begins with God's acceptance of me through Christ must be extended in terms of loving, forgiving acceptance of my fellowmen around me. Then, truly, I can celebrate, and in celebrating, I may reflect something of the joy of heaven amidst the agony and ugliness of this world.

7

Can I Forgive—
And Serve?

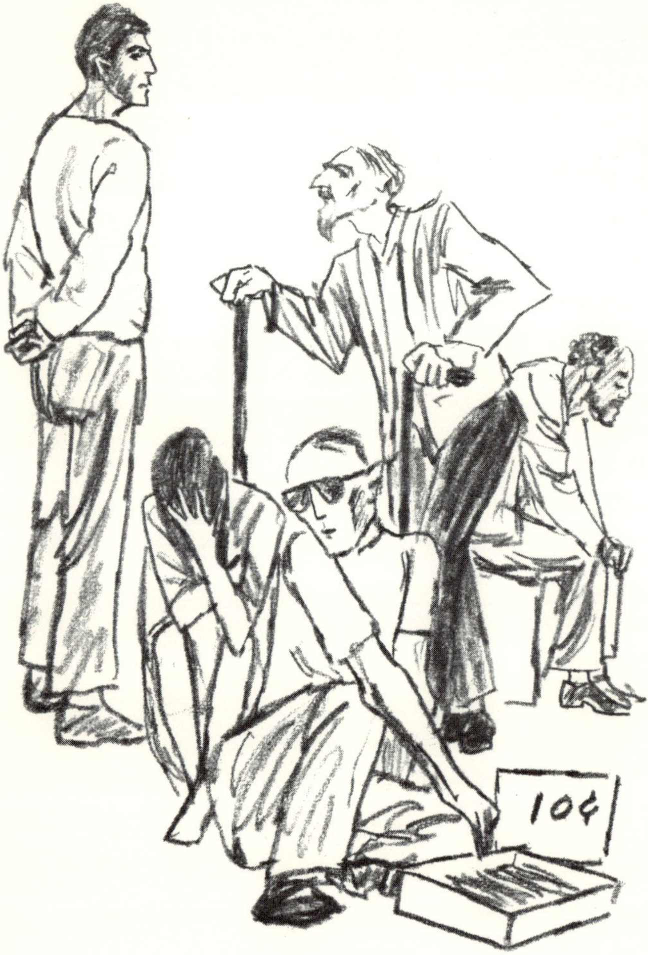
10¢

THE CROSS, as a symbol of the Christian faith, is a remarkable picture of Christianity's content and meaning. It has often been used to portray our vertical and horizontal relationships to God and fellowman.

Its vertical shaft speaks to me about divine forgiveness and the reconciliation that has been effected between God and me through Jesus Christ. I need but to accept His eternal love and rest in His everlasting pardon. It is a fact accomplished, a relationship secured. I am His son forever.

The horizontal shaft is as much a part of that cross as is the vertical. It is this that speaks to me about my relationship to my fellowman. The cross is a reiteration as well as a fulfillment of God's original love-God-love-your-neighbor injunction to mankind. It has been my discovery that the vertical cannot be separated from the horizontal. They are welded into a single unit and represent a single and perpetual experience.

It says, in essence, that if I am to remain rightly related to God, I must constantly seek out and persistently promote right relationships to my fellowmen. It is true that my horizontal relationships are to be a consequence of and a response to my vertical relationship — my relationship to God. It is also apparent that this demands a commitment on my part, a commitment to the needs and concerns of my fellowmen.

I have never realized this so acutely as I have in the last decade. My Christian upbringing put great emphasis on the vertical relationship, which was interpreted largely in terms of "love" feelings toward Jesus Christ and "peace" feelings in respect to personal forgiveness and life after death. I got the impression that my horizontal relationships or responsibilities were fulfilled in simply preaching or witnessing to others concerning my faith and in trying to get them to accept Jesus Christ.

I continue to believe that my goal is to bring God to man and man to God through faith in Christ the Redeemer. As my faith has become more dynamic, however, my concern for helping my fellowman also in his physical needs has increased. In other words, I am called to fulfill my commission of being a servant to my neighbor—to show love and concern, to meet him and minister to him at the point of his need. This means that, as the opportunity arises, I must speak the Gospel to him and also demonstrate it by deeds of love. Actually, such a demonstration of the love that God pours out upon His creatures often precedes proclamation. It may set the stage for proclamation—if not by me, then through the lips of others.

Luther taught that our neighbor is God's representative in this world who is appointed by God to receive the sacrifices of love and service which are to be offered to God through the neighbor. A Christian is a channel, open upwards to heaven by faith (vertical), and outwards to the neighbor through love (horizontal). A Christian, according to Luther, is called to be Christ to his neighbor. Our neighbor represents the invisible Christ. Whereas the Old Testament worshipers offered their sacrifices on stone altars, New Testament worshipers are to offer their sacrifices to God by way of the altar of their neighbor's need.

It becomes very apparent that I must forgive my fellowman before I can effectively and creatively serve him. It is not as easy as it sounds—to forgive and then to truly love and accept my fellowman as my equal. One reason for this is that my forgiveness of others tends to be shallow and condescending. In the act of forgiving others it is natural to put myself on a higher plane—as if I am holier or kinder or more loving and generous than are those whom I forgive.

God's forgiveness, manifested through Christ and brought to us by the Holy Spirit through Word and Sacrament, certainly came from One who is holier and more loving than any of His creatures who daily cross Him up. And yet Christ stooped from His high position to identify with sinful, suffering humanity, to become one with them, and then to suffer degrading, torturous death on that atrocious instrument of execution on humanity's behalf.

I can't begin to fathom this divine act of reconciliation. But it does point up something of the meaning of forgiveness in respect to my relationships to my fellowmen. I share in and am an integral part of every man's sin. I must, in some sense of the word, identify with those I forgive. In the process of forgiving and accepting and loving them, I forgive and accept and love myself. And all this takes place only by virtue of God's eternal love and perpetual grace poured out upon me and my fellowmen.

Celebration and service are twin

sisters. As God's forgiveness results in my ability to forgive others and sets me free to celebrate, so it sets me free to serve. In fact, forgiveness is not genuinely received nor given unless it resolves in both celebration and service. One can serve without really acknowledging and rejoicing in God's forgiveness, but it is service stifled, limited, and usually without the healing power of true love. It is the rigid letter of the Law rather than the life-giving effervescence of the Spirit. It is the vain attempt to gain credits rather than the gracious sharing of divine gifts already received.

I am called to serve. I am called to serve creatively. God through Christ is creativity incarnate. His life, through the power of the Spirit, is the proper content of my life. It may be possible to serve humanity even while bound in the tentacles of sin and self-centeredness. But until I am set free from such—and from the hostility and animosity I harbor toward others—it is highly unlikely that I can serve creatively. How often my own ministry has been stymied by guilt and hostility! On the other hand, when I am truly open to God and my fellowman, I do sense God's Spirit doing creative things in the lives of people in my path.

This is the life-style of a child of God—to be set free to celebrate and to serve.

> *O God, now I know who I am.*
> *I am Your servant.*
> *I am to serve You in serving my brothers about me.*
> *I do not know my future course,*
>   *but I know where I am now.*
> *Through the pressure of circumstances*
>   *or the persuasion of Your loving control,*
>   *I am here to serve my fellowman,*
>   *to retain and further comprehend my identity*
>   *in losing my life in behalf of others.*
>
> *I thank You, O God,*
>   *for making me valid and significant,*
>   *for putting meaning into my life and purpose into my living,*

*for snatching me out of the pit of self-centeredness
and restoring my identity as a member
of Your eternal family. Amen.*